Hernando de Soto

and the Exploration
of Florida

Hernando de Soto

and the Exploration of Florida

Jim Gallagher

Chelsea House Publishers
Philadelphia

The author wishes to thank Marian and Harry Hartpence for their assistance in the preparation of this book. I couldn't have done it without you!

Prepared for Chelsea House Publishers by:
OTTN Publishing, Warminster, PA

CHELSEA HOUSE PUBLISHERS
Editor in Chief: Stephen Reginald
Managing Editor: James D. Gallagher
Production Manager: Pamela Loos
Art Director: Sara Davis
Director of Photography: Judy L. Hasday
Senior Production Editor: LeeAnne Gelletly
Series Designer: Keith Trego

First Printing
1 3 5 7 9 8 6 4 2

Library of Congress Cataloging-in-Publication Data

Gallagher, Jim, 1969–
    Hernando de Soto and the exploration of Florida / by
    Jim Gallagher.
    p.   cm. – (Explorers of new worlds)
Includes bibliographical references and index.
Summary: A biography of the wealthy Spaniard who came to the New World to seek glory and who was the first European to reach the Mississippi River in 1541.
ISBN 0-7910-5512-4
1. Soto, Hernando de, ca. 1500–1542 Juvenile literature. 2. Explorers–America Biography Juvenile literature. 3. Explorers–Spain Biography Juvenile literature. 4. Florida–Discovery and exploration–Florida Juvenile literature. 5. Florida–History–To 1565 Juvenile literature. 6. America–Discovery and exploration–Spanish Juvenile literature.[1. De Soto, Hernando, ca. 1500–1542. 2. Explorers. 3. America–Discovery and exploration–Spanish.] I. Title. II. Series.
E125.S7G06   1999
970.1'5'092–dc21

                                                            99-22257
                                                            CIP

Contents

Shortly after the Spanish soldiers arrived in Florida, they were surprised to find a man who spoke their language. Juan Ortiz was a survivor of a previous expedition to Florida.

God, Gold, and Glory   I

he Spanish scouting party marched through an open field, on the lookout for danger. Suddenly, the armored soldiers spotted four dark-skinned natives. The Spaniards charged at the Indians, shouting their battle cry: "Santiago!"

Just a few days earlier, the men had landed in the unexplored land they called *La Florida*. They were members of an expedition led by Hernando de Soto. He had been granted permission by King Charles of Spain to create a colony in Florida. De Soto and his men were hoping to find gold as they journeyed through the territory.

As the soldiers surrounded them, one of the frightened natives raised his hands and shouted in Spanish. Then he made the sign of the cross. This startled the attackers. They had thought all of the natives were **heathens**, uncivilized people who did not believe in God. In fact, one of their missions was to convert the Indians to Christianity. Now, here was a man who spoke their language and knew their religion. The Spaniards halted their attack.

The strange man, it turned out, *was* Spanish. He was hard to understand, because he had lived among the Indians for many years. The man told the soldiers that his name was Juan Ortiz. He had been a member of an earlier Spanish expedition to Florida, but had been left behind.

The Spaniards escorted him to their nearby camp. When Ortiz was brought before Hernando de Soto, he told his story. Eleven years earlier, the leader of his expedition, Pánfilo de Narváez, had angered the local **cacique**, or native chief, whose name was Hirrihigua. Narváez had cut off the chief's nose and ordered his mother to be killed. When Hirrihigua's men attacked, the Spanish were forced to sail away. Four men were captured by the natives. Fifteen-year-old Juan Ortiz was one of them.

The cacique ordered the four men to be roasted alive over hot coals. The first three men were killed in this horrible way. Juan Ortiz would have died the same way, except that the cacique's wife and daughters pitied the teenager. While he screamed in agony at the searing pain, they begged the chief to spare his life. Hirrihigua finally agreed to let the boy go, but not before Ortiz's skin was badly blistered.

Although Juan Ortiz was allowed to live, the cacique was still angry. Hirrihigua often kicked and beat Ortiz as revenge for his own *mutilation*. Hirrihigua's daughter was afraid Ortiz would be killed one day. She told him how to get to a village where he would be safe.

When Ortiz reached the village, the cacique, Mocozo, made him a member of the Timucuan tribe. Ortiz spent 11 years with the Indians. When the Native Americans spotted the masts of de Soto's ships landing in the harbor, Chief Mocozo sent Ortiz and some guides to meet the Spaniards.

De Soto and the other men were amazed at the story. During his years in Florida, Ortiz had learned several native languages. Because he could talk with the Indians, De Soto asked him to join the party as an *interpreter*. Ortiz happily accepted.

When de Soto's men landed in Florida, they stayed in huts like these in the village of Ucita for several months, before leaving Ucita to search for gold.

Hernando de Soto's next question was about the tribe Ortiz had been living with. Did they have any gold or silver? The Spanish had come to start a colony and to convert the heathen Indians, but they also wanted to become rich. De Soto had promised King Charles that he would find riches for Spain in the unexplored wilderness.

Ever since he was a child, de Soto had heard tales about seven Spanish bishops. According to the stories, the bishops and their congregations had left

Spain after it was invaded by the **Moors**, a tribe of Moslems from North Africa, around 750 A.D. They built boats and traveled west across the Atlantic Ocean. When they reached land, the exiled bishops established seven glorious cities and filled them with riches. These became known as the Seven Cities of Gold. Hernando de Soto was sure that the Seven Cities were located somewhere in Florida, and he intended to find them.

Juan Ortiz's answer was disappointing. The Timucuan tribe that had sheltered him did not have gold or valuables. However, there were rumors of a powerful tribe that lived to the north. Perhaps they had gold, or knew where to find it.

De Soto was not discouraged. He had persevered in a three-year search for wealth in South America, returning to his native country as one of the richest men in Spain. Florida was large, and the Seven Cities of Gold could be anywhere.

De Soto's men knew their commander was stubborn and bold. They also respected him for his toughness and his loyalty to his soldiers. Despite the swamps and mosquitoes, they had placed their trust in the dark-haired leader. They would follow wherever he commanded, searching for gold in Florida.

A Conquistador
Is Born

The Spanish explorer Vasco Núñez de Balboa views the Pacific Ocean, the first time a European had seen the great body of water. Balboa was a neighbor of Hernando de Soto's in Spain, and de Soto followed the older conquistador to the Spanish colony in Central America.

2

ernando de Soto was born around the year 1500. His parents lived in the town of Jerez de los Caballeros, which was located in the mountains of central Spain. Both Hernando's mother and father were of royal blood. His older brother decided to follow a Spanish custom of the time and use both his parents' names: Juan Méndez de Soto. Hernando decided to be different. He was his mother's favorite, so when he grew older he dropped the Méndez from his name. He would gain fame with the name Hernando de Soto.

There is a legend that when Hernando was nine years old, a neighbor stopped him one day. The man showed him flakes of gold, telling Hernando, "If you don't have this, you don't have anything."

This story may or may not be true. But de Soto's inspiration to find gold and glory may have been a neighbor named Vasco Núñez de Balboa. When de Soto was about 13 years old, Balboa led an exploring party from Darién, a small Spanish colony in the New World, across the *isthmus* of Panama. Balboa discovered a great body of water that he named the South Sea. Today, Balboa's South Sea is better known as the Pacific Ocean.

Another Spanish *conquistador*, Juan Ponce de León, also gained fame in 1513. Ponce de León discovered a new land a few miles north of Cuba. He named the region *Pascua Florida* (Easter of Flowers).

De Soto admired both men and wished to match their accomplishments. In 1514 he left Jerez for the important city of Seville. There, he joined the service of Pedro Arias Dávila. When Dávila was appointed *adelantado*, or governor, of the Darién colony, de Soto got his chance to sail to the New World.

The sun sets over a river in Darién, Panama, where the Spanish established a colony in the 16th century. Darién probably looked a lot like this when 15-year-old Hernando de Soto arrived there around 1514.

As a soldier for Dávila, de Soto quickly earned a reputation for bravery and stubbornness. He often led the soldiers of Darién in bold raids against the natives of Central America. He earned gold and Indian slaves for his role in these successful attacks.

In 1523, there was trouble in the New World.

De Soto was second in command of the army, serving under Francisco Fernández de Córdoba. When there was unrest in a neighboring colony, Dávila sent Córdoba and his men to replace its leader. But Córdoba decided to take control of the *province* himself, against Dávila's wishes.

Hernando de Soto remained loyal to his *patron* Dávila and opposed Córdoba's plans. The general ordered de Soto to be imprisoned, but the resourceful leader escaped with the help of a friend named Francisco Companion. He and eight others who did not support the rebellious general fled the camp and trekked back to Darién.

Upon hearing the news, Dávila sent troops to capture Córdoba. The Spanish general was brought back to Darién in chains. Córdoba was convicted of *treason* and executed.

Hernando de Soto always followed Pedro Arias Dávila's orders— even when he didn't like them. In 1519, Dávila had ordered Balboa to be executed because he disputed the leadership of the colony. Even though de Soto liked and respected Balboa, he carried out Dávila's orders. Afterward, a sad de Soto arranged for his friend's funeral.

Hernando Cortés gained great wealth and fame by conquering the vast Aztec empire with a small army. His adventures inspired men like Francisco Pizarro, as well as de Soto himself.

Despite this incident, Darién was prospering and so was de Soto. In fact, the New World had turned out to be a place where brave Spanish explorers could become rich. In 1519 a Spanish general named Hernando Cortés had landed in Mexico. Cortés led a 500-man army to Tenochtitlán, the capital of the powerful Aztec Empire.

There were approximately 3 million Aztecs, and their armies vastly outnumbered the Spaniards. However, Cortés's men were armed with steel swords and pikes, powerful crossbows, and even a type of gun called an ***arquebus***. These weapons were far superior to the stone-tipped spears and arrows used by the Aztec warriors. And the conquistadors rode strange animals the Aztecs had never seen before: horses.

An Aztec legend also helped the Spanish. The natives thought Cortés was a god and could not be defeated. Their leader, Montezuma, was afraid to attack until he learned more about these strange white-skinned invaders. By the time he decided to resist, it was too late. Cortés's Spanish soldiers captured Montezuma and took control of Tenochtitlán.

The huge Aztec Empire would not be easily subdued. It took three difficult years of fighting both the natives and the jungles of Mexico. However, for Cortés and his men the reward was great. The Aztecs had large supplies of gold and silver. Cortés returned to Spain in triumph, second only to King Charles in wealth.

This success inspired other soldiers to search for gold in the New World. In 1528, a 52-year-old explorer named Francisco Pizarro asked the king if he could lead an expedition into South America.

Pizarro had been a member of Balboa's party that had discovered the Pacific. In 1527, one of his ships had captured several natives on a raft. The men, members of the Inca tribe, had a box of gold and silver jewelry and precious stones on their small boat. Pizarro believed the Incas had a great treasure hoard and decided to look for it.

The Incas called themselves "Children of the Sun." They ruled an empire that was as large as the Aztecs'. It extended for 2,000 miles along the west coast of South America. The Inca Empire stretched from the mountainous heart of the continent in northern Ecuador to the middle of Chile.

Pizarro was granted permission from the king to invade the Inca Empire in 1529. He agreed to give one-fifth of any riches he found to Charles, and to convert the natives to Christianity. Pizarro invited de Soto to join his army. By this time, Hernando de Soto was so rich that he was able to provide two ships and a company of soldiers and horses. He took the rank of captain.

The ruins of an Incan city in the mountains of Peru. Under Pizarro and Hernando de Soto, the Spaniards crossed a vast area of South America seeking the riches of the Inca Empire.

Conquest of the Incas 3

izarro's troop of 180 men and 67 horses left Darién early in 1531. They were armed with arquebuses, swords, long lances, crossbows, and two cannons.

When the Spaniards landed in South America, they were constantly harassed by the native warriors. However, the Indians were no match for the conquistadors. The natives were especially frightened by the horses. No South American had ever seen a horse before. They thought the swift four-legged animals were magical creatures.

For a year, the Spaniards journeyed south, establishing two settlements, Paita and San Miguel.

When the Spanish soldiers captured some natives, Pizarro learned that the Inca Empire was divided. The ruler of the Incas had died six years earlier, leaving the kingdom to his two sons, Atahualpa and Huascar. They had ruled together for five years, but a disagreement had occurred that caused a *civil war*. The Spaniards were pleased to hear that the Incas were fighting each other.

In September of 1532, Pizarro learned that Atahualpa had captured his brother and was in control of the empire. He and de Soto set out with their men for the city of Cajamarca. The city was 300 miles to the south. The journey was hard, and some of the men grumbled. It was hot, dry, and dusty. Also, they did not know what to expect. No European had ever traveled this deep into Peru.

At the Indian city of Cajas, de Soto met a messenger from Atahualpa. He brought the man back to Pizarro's camp. The messenger gave Pizarro some gifts and said that Atahualpa wanted the Spanish to visit him in peace. However, de Soto thought the man might be a spy. He seemed very interested in the Spaniards' numbers and in their weapons.

The Inca led Pizarro's expedition to Cajamarca. The Spaniards had to cross the Sechura Desert.

They marched for three days through the sandy wilderness. When they finally reached water, the men leapt into the Leche River. Then they started over the Andes Mountains. The Spaniards were not used to the high altitude, and many became sick. Also, the roads were narrow. It would have been easy for the Incas to ambush Pizarro, but they did not attack.

When the Spanish reached Cajamarca, they were amazed. The city was deserted, but Atahualpa and 40,000 soldiers were camped outside. Pizarro and his officers were concerned. Was the small Spanish force going to be ambushed?

Pizarro decided the best thing would be for the Spaniards to march into the abandoned city. "It was unwise to show any fear," he later wrote. "We had to go into the town. So with a show of good spirits, we descended into the valley. . . . The most sensible course was to make as bold an appearance as possible and continue openly without any apparent fear or regard for the Incas."

After the Spaniards settled into the city, Pizarro sent de Soto and some mounted soldiers to visit Atahualpa. De Soto knew that Indians were afraid of the horses, so he rode as close to their leader as he could. One of the soldiers later wrote that the breath from de Soto's horse stirred the fringe on Atahualpa's headdress, but the ruler did not flinch. "One squadron of troops drew back when they saw the horse coming toward them," he wrote. "Those who did this paid for it that night with their lives, for Atahualpa ordered them to be killed because they had shown fear."

While Atahualpa and his warriors were watching de Soto's men, Pizarro came up with a bold plan to capture the Inca ruler. The natives worshipped Atahualpa as though he were a god. Pizarro believed that if he could take Atahualpa prisoner, the Indians would surrender to the Spaniards.

When de Soto returned, Pizarro outlined his plan. He placed de Soto in charge of half of the cavalry. The rest was commanded by the general's half-brother, Hernando Pizarro. Their forces were hidden on either side of the plaza. Pizarro placed his cannons and troops armed with crossbows and arquebuses on top of a temple that overlooked the open square. He and a group of 20 men would wait for Atahualpa inside the plaza.

The next day, the conquistadors waited all day for Atahualpa to appear. Finally, as the sun began to

*W*hy were Pizarro and the Spanish interested in conquering the Incas? The answer is simple—gold. The Incas did have many gold and silver ornaments, such as the toucan pictured above, which is decorated with emeralds, and the hammered gold mask at right. The natives of Peru had also developed an incredibly complex civilization. But with the com-

ing of the Spanish conquistadors, the Inca Empire was destroyed, and many gold items like these were melted down and shipped back to Spain.

set, a procession of Incas marched into the town. Many of the men were wearing large gold ornaments. Atahualpa was riding on a **litter**, or platform, carried by 80 men. Behind him came several hundred of his best troops.

When Pizarro gave the signal, the cannons were fired at the Indian forces. The attack threw the Incas into confusion. Then de Soto and Hernando Pizarro, shouting battle cries, led their mounted troops into the fray. At the same time, Francisco Pizarro led his 20 soldiers across the square, fighting through Atahualpa's guard until they grasped the Inca ruler. Seeing their leader captured, the demoralized Indians broke and ran from the battlefield. De Soto chased the fleeing Inca warriors with his cavalry.

In 30 minutes, the defeat of the Incas was complete. Five thousand Indians had been killed. There were no Spanish casualties.

The next day, the Spanish put some captives to work dragging corpses out of the city. De Soto led a group of men to the Inca camp and returned with a large amount of gold. Atahualpa saw how excited the Spaniards were about the gold. He promised to fill a room with gold and two rooms with silver, if

When Atahualpa was captured, Incan resistance melted away. Fearing for his life, the ruler promised to give the Spaniards a room full of gold if they would spare him.

the conquistadors spared his life.

For nine months, Atahualpa was held captive while this ransom was assembled. During this time he learned how to read and write in Spanish, played chess with Pizarro, and was treated as royalty. At last, 24 tons of gold had been collected.

Even though Atahualpa had kept his end of the bargain, Pizarro was afraid that the Inca ruler would try to stir up a revolt. He forced Atahualpa to publicly convert to Christianity, and then strangled the Inca ruler on August 29, 1533.

Despite the death of their leader, the Incas continued to resist. One of Atahualpa's top soldiers, Rumiñahui, led the attacks on Pizarro's men as they moved toward another important Inca city, Cuzco.

On November 2, 1533, the Spanish army was defeated for the first time. De Soto and a group of horsemen had stopped to rest along a steep mountain pass known as Vilcaconga. Suddenly, a barrage of stones dropped on his men from the hills above. Then, an army of native soldiers ran down the hill toward them. The Spaniards had to retreat, and many were killed. Some of the horses were killed also. This showed the Indians that the animals were not invincible.

Despite this knowledge, the Inca warriors were no match for the Spaniards. On November 15 they captured Cuzco. Pizarro rewarded de Soto for his loyal service by placing him in charge of the city.

All of the men who had fought with Pizarro, even the lowest foot soldier, became exceptionally rich

De Soto did not want to see Atahualpa killed. He wanted to send him to King Charles in Spain instead. Pizarro waited until de Soto was away on a raid to rid himself of the Inca ruler.

Hernando de Soto leads a group of Spanish horsemen along a narrow mountain pass. The Battle of Vilcaconga Pass showed the Incas that the Spanish soldiers and their horses could be beaten. However, the invaders were too strong and well-equipped for the native warriors, and defeated the Inca army within a few weeks.

because of the expedition's success. King Charles's share was 2,700 pounds of gold, and he received even more in silver and emeralds. Francisco Pizarro took 800 pounds of gold for himself. He gave de Soto more than 200 pounds of gold and 400 pounds of silver. This made the brave soldier one of the richest men in the world.

Hernando de Soto spent four years as lieutenant governor of Cuzco. In 1535, he decided to return to Spain. When he had left 21 years earlier, he was just a teenager in search of adventure. Now, the returning conquistador was greeted as a hero.

Members of the Hernando de Soto Historical Society re-create the Spanish conquistador's landing on the Florida coast in 1539. The actual landing site is disputed.

The Exploration of *La Florida* 4

ernando de Soto's adventures in the New World had provided enough wealth for him to retire to a life of luxury. He purchased a large house in Seville and hired servants. He gave generously to his friends and even loaned money to the king. De Soto also married Isabel de Bobadilla, the daughter of his friend Pedro Arias Dávila.

However, de Soto was only 36 years old. He felt that he was too young to retire. He craved action. He also wanted the glory that comes with leading an expedition of discovery. All his life, he had been second in command. Now, de Soto felt, it was his turn to be in charge.

King Charles I of Spain did not give de Soto permission to invade an unexplored area of South America, because there were already several strong-willed leaders there. He was afraid that his best soldiers would wind up fighting each other for control of the continent. He ordered de Soto instead to "conquer, pacify, and popu-late" La Florida.

After a few months in Seville, de Soto asked King Charles for permission to conquer another area of South America. The king asked him instead to explore an enormous unexplored land north of Cuba. He was to establish a colony and look for gold and silver. If de Soto was successful, the king promised to give him hundreds of acres of land, along with a rich annual salary. He also placed de Soto in charge of Spain's colony in Cuba.

The region that King Charles wanted explored had been named *La Florida* by Juan Ponce de León in 1513. It stretched north as far as the Carolinas, and as far west as the river that separates present-day Texas from Mexico. (The Spanish called this the Rio de las Palmas. Today, it is better known as the Rio Grande.)

Many people wanted to join de Soto's expedition. They felt sure he would find gold in Florida. De Soto selected about 700 men to join his expedition. Most were soldiers, but the party also included several priests and friars, tailors, shoemakers, a swordsmith, and a *farrier* who could make shoes for the Spaniards' horses.

In April 1538, de Soto's fleet of eight ships left Spain. The fleet reached Havana, Cuba, by the end of May. There, they purchased food, tools, weapons, and items that they could use to trade with the natives: knives, mirrors, and beads.

The Spaniards purchased 230 horses to take to the colony in Florida, along with hunting dogs. The men also brought a herd of long-legged hogs. These could be used as a mobile food supply.

Hernando de Soto knew it was important to find a good landing area. While his men waited on

Cuba, de Soto sent several small scouting parties to the Florida coast. It was about a year before he felt prepared to begin exploring. His ships set out for Florida in May 1539. The men landed on May 30, probably somewhere in the area of Tampa Bay, although the exact location is unknown.

A few days after landing in Florida, the Spaniards encountered Juan Ortiz. Ortiz had been living with the Timucuan Indian tribe ruled by Mocozo. When de Soto heard about the chief's kindness toward Ortiz, he gave gifts to Mocozo. The Spanish and the Timucuans coexisted peacefully. However, other native tribes did not trust the Spanish invaders. They generally tried to avoid de Soto's army, but they attacked his scouts constantly.

The *guerrilla* tactics of the Indians, who fired deadly arrows while hidden in the swamps, annoyed the Spaniards. In Europe, war was much simpler. The two armies lined up against each other and fought until one side gave up. The Spaniards' armor and weapons were not suited to swamp warfare. A native could fire three arrows and disappear in the time it took a Spanish soldier to fire and reload his arquebus once. Also, the Florida heat was very uncomfortable for men wearing suits of armor.

Many people believe that de Soto and his men landed at this Florida beach on Tampa Bay. The expedition's actual landing site is uncertain, however.

The Spaniards camped in an abandoned Indian village called Ucita. De Soto sent his scouts to look for other Indian villages. When they found them, they asked where gold could be found. No one seemed to know for sure, but there were many rumors about a tribe that lived in the northwest province of Cale. De Soto was told that the tribe had an abundance of maize and grain, and the warriors of Cale wore helmets of gold.

In mid-July 1539, de Soto and 500 of his men set out to find the gold. He left about 100 men in the fortified city of Ucita. They were commanded by Pedro Calderón. The men had a two-year supply of food. De Soto promised Calderón that if he discovered a better place to settle, he would let them know. The adelantado also sent five of his eight ships back to Cuba. He told the captains to bring supplies and new recruits back to Florida.

There had been heavy rains that year, and the Spanish soldiers struggled through swampy land. In some cases, they had to build bridges over swollen streams. They herded the pigs that they had brought from Cuba as food. They also lived off the land, killing the local wildlife whenever possible or taking grain when they found Indian villages. As they marched, the invaders continued to be harassed by the Native Americans.

Finally, de Soto's men reached Cale. The Spaniards found plenty of **maize**, beans, and other food—but no gold. Undaunted, de Soto ordered his men to load themselves with enough grain to last for three months. The natives were angry at being robbed of their harvest, and they attacked and killed three of the Spaniards.

After fighting off the Indian attack, Hernando de Soto split his force. He left most of the men at the camp under the command of Luis Moscoso de Alvarado and rode ahead with a group scouts. In mid-August, de Soto's men captured 20 prisoners, including a chief and his daughter, at a village called Aguacaliquen. He sent orders to Moscoso, telling him to bring the rest of the men to Aguacaliquen. Then, he forced the chief and other Indian prisoners to guide the Spaniards to the next village.

The Spaniards and their captives arrived at the village of Napituca on September 15, 1539. In three months, they had traveled over 200 miles through the uncharted wilderness. De Soto and his weary soldiers were pleased to hear that the cacique of the village, Vitachuco, had prepared a feast for the Spaniards. Finally, they could relax.

But the Spaniards could not relax for long. Juan Ortiz, who understood the native language, overheard Vitachuco planning a surprise attack. He warned de Soto, who prepared his men to be ready for the ambush.

The next day, Vitachuco invited de Soto to review his warriors on a plain outside the village. The Indian warriors had hidden their weapons in

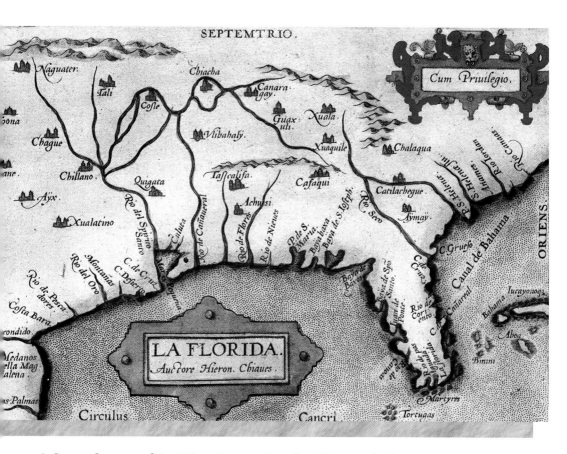

A Spanish map of La Florida, *made after Hernando de Soto's expedition, shows the location of many of the Native American villages that he and his men visited.*

the grass. De Soto's men followed as he walked into the field with Vitachuco. Suddenly, the Spanish leader signaled his men to attack! De Soto then leapt onto a horse and led a charge at the warriors.

After months of frustrating skirmishes, the Spaniards were eager for a battle in the open field. They quickly routed Vitachuco's 400-man army.

About 40 Indians were killed by the Spaniards' long lances and arquebuses, and hundreds were captured, including the treacherous cacique.

De Soto gave gifts to some of the captured Indians—the ones he felt had shown great bravery in the battle—and set them free. The Spanish intended to keep the rest as guides or to carry their food and equipment. However, the adelantado treated Vitachuco well, even inviting the cacique to have dinner with him in the village.

One night, after Vitachuco finished eating, he surprised de Soto by leaping at him. The cacique punched the conquistador in the face, knocking him unconscious, before the Spanish soldiers recovered from their shock and pulled him off their leader.

This attack sparked the captured Indians to revolt throughout the village. They grasped any weapons they could find to fight the Spanish soldiers: pots, blazing sticks from cooking fires, rocks, and plates. For several hours, the soldiers defended themselves against the 200 rebellious natives. Finally, the uprising was quelled. Some of the Indians, including Vitachuco, were killed. Others were enslaved by the Spanish, who chained them together with iron collars.

On September 23, de Soto's men set out for Apalache territory. Along the way, the natives continued to harass the Spanish force, which reached the village of Anhaica in October. Anhaica was abandoned, because word had spread about the Spaniards. The Spanish built a wooden fence around the village and planned to spend the winter.

> **Anhaica, a village of 250 houses, was located where the present-day city of Tallahassee stands. De Soto's men found a large supply of corn, pumpkins, squash, and maize that helped them survive the winter.**

De Soto sent some of his men to find the ocean, which he knew was nearby. Although the scouts were led astray by their Indian guide, eventually they discovered a bay. When de Soto learned about this inlet, he sent 30 of his horsemen, under Juan de Añasco, back to the settlement at Ucita. De Soto wanted Pedro Calderón to bring the 100 men from the Ucita settlement to Anhaica.

The Spanish horsemen had a dangerous mission. They had to retrace the long journey that they had just made, through territory filled with hostile natives. The horsemen managed to avoid the Indians and reach Ucita in October.

De Soto ordered Calderón to send the smallest ship, called a ***caravel***, back to Cuba with a message for his wife. The other two ships would be sailed to the harbor where de Soto and his men were encamped. The ships would carry equipment and men. Those who could not fit on the two ***brigantines*** would have to march to the camp, guided by de Soto's weary horsemen.

The ships reached de Soto's camp in November, and the marching soldiers reached Anhaica the next month. De Soto then sent the ships west. He placed Francisco Maldonado in charge of an expedition to find a protected bay, where supplies and new soldiers from Cuba could meet his force.

All winter, the Spaniards asked the natives where they could find gold or silver in Florida. One captive Indian told Juan Ortiz that a rich country lay to the northeast. The captive, whom the Spanish nicknamed Perico, said that Cofitachequi, as the country was called, was located near the rising sun. It was ruled by a female cacique who was respected by many powerful chiefs. Listening to his stories, the Spaniards felt sure that great wealth was nearly in their grasp—wealth that would outshine that of the Aztecs and the Incas.

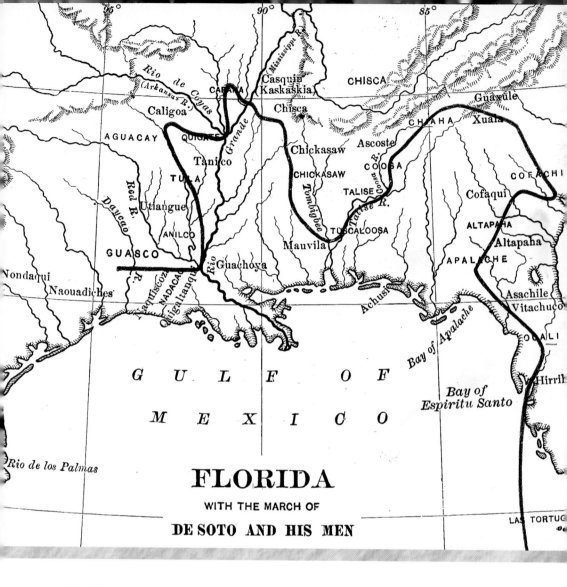

FLORIDA

WITH THE MARCH OF

DE SOTO AND HIS MEN

Wandering in the Wilderness

This map shows the wandering path that Hernando de Soto and his men took in looking for gold in Florida. The names of Indian tribes that the Spaniards encountered, and the rulers that they visited, are marked on the map.

5

*I*n March 1540, de Soto and his men left Anhaica, traveling north. Most of their captured native slaves had died over the winter. This meant the Spaniards had to carry all their supplies and make their own meals. The going was difficult, and many of the streams were swollen from spring rains.

After two days, the soldiers stopped at the Capacheguy River. It was too wide to cross. De Soto's men built barges and strung a cable over the river so that they could pull their horses and equipment to the other side.

Their northward march took them through the present-day states of Georgia and South Carolina. Here, the Spanish encountered Indians of a new tribe, the Creek. The Europeans admired the natives' clean cabins and their colorful, dyed clothing. The Creek also were less hostile than other Indians had been. They provided food to the expedition, and some served willingly as guides.

After nearly two months of hard traveling, however, friendly natives and food were becoming scarce. The main guide was Perico, who had told the Spaniards about the treasure-filled city of Cofitachequi. He finally admitted that he was lost. This made de Soto very angry. It was not until the adelantado's scouts came into contact with some natives who knew the area that the party received good directions to the village. It was about 25 miles away.

When the explorers reached the Savannah River, they were met by a woman surrounded by attendants. The woman was the cacique of Cofitachequi, and she gracefully invited de Soto and his men to stay in her village. "Be this coming to these shores most happy," she told de Soto. "With sincerest and purest good will, I tender you my person, my lands, [and] my people." The Spaniards were impressed and named her *La Señora de Cofitachequi*–the Lady of Cofitachequi.

When they reached the village, the explorers found that the cacique had sent half of the tribe away so that there would be room for the visitors to stay. She told the explorers that they could take grain, asking only that they leave half of the tribe's stockpile. The Spaniards asked the Indians about gold, but once again they were disappointed. The natives offered the party what they had–copper and 350 pounds of pearls.

The soldiers wanted to divide the pearls, but de Soto wanted his men to keep their packs empty so that they could be filled with gold when it was found. He took 50 pounds of pearls in a chest to give to King Charles, and allowed each man to take two handfuls.

As a friendship gesture, the Lady of Cofitachequi gave Hernando de Soto her necklace. It was "a large strand of pearls as thick as hazelnuts which encircled her neck three times and fell to her thighs," a member of the party wrote. In return, de Soto took a gold-and-ruby ring off his finger and handed it to her.

De Soto, wearing a fancy hat with a white feather, leads his men on the march through Florida. Some historians believe de Soto was flamboyant and cocky, but there is no question that he was also brave and determined.

The men enjoyed the hospitality of La Señora de Cofitachequi. The weather was nice, and the land was beautiful. Some of the Spaniards wanted to settle there. However, de Soto urged them on, reminding them of the gold and glory that lay ahead. While in Cofitachequi, he had heard rumors about a tribe to the northwest that possessed gold.

When Hernando de Soto and his men set out, they brought La Señora de Cofitachequi with them—

against her will. Some of her people also went along
as porters. The expedition turned to the west, into
the Appalachian Mountains and present-day North
Carolina. There, the cacique of Cofitachequi and
her men slipped away, after traveling hundreds of
miles from their village. They took de Soto's chest
of pearls with them.

Without guides, de Soto's men wandered
through the unknown wilderness. They crossed the
Appalachian mountain range and moved north to
the present-day city of Knoxville, Tennessee. Then,
the explorers turned south.

The Spaniards passed through the native villages
of Coosa and Itaba, traveling down the Coosa River
toward the Gulf of Mexico. Each time they entered
an Indian town, they captured its leaders and took
them along as guides to the next town. They also
forced Indians to carry their equipment. As the party
continued south, the Spaniards captured a powerful
chief named Tascaluza. The chief pretended to be
awed by the Spaniards. He provided 100 native
porters. But secretly, he sent word ahead to his
town, Mabila, to prepare an ambush.

As the party neared Mabila in mid-October of
1540, some of de Soto's soldiers warned their leader

to be cautious. They had seen Indians bringing extra food into the village and strengthening a **palisade**, or wooden fence, that surrounded Mabila. But de Soto felt safe when messengers from the town brought him bread made from chestnuts. He decided to lead a small group of horsemen into town. This, he felt sure, would make the natives think twice about attacking.

De Soto was wrong. When the Spanish entered the town, they were unexpectedly attacked by thousands of Indians. Staggered by a deadly hail of arrows and spears, the Spaniards quickly withdrew. During the confusion, the Indians who had been carrying food and equipment for the Spaniards ran into the village with the supplies. The conquistadors would need to get their supplies back to survive.

An angry de Soto rallied his men. The Spaniards attacked the town from all sides and soon set it on fire. The fighting raged for five hours. "The struggle lasted so long that many Christians, weary and very thirsty, went to drink at a pond near by, tinged with the blood of the killed, and returned to combat," wrote one soldier who survived the expedition.

The Indians were no match for the superior weapons and fighting skills of the conquistadors. At least 2,500 natives were killed in the struggle. On the Spanish side, 22 men were dead and about 150 were wounded. De Soto was one of them. He had been hit by an arrow, but the wound was not serious.

Nonetheless, the daylong battle was a disaster for the Spanish. A lot of their equipment had been destroyed when the town went up in flames. Also, 80 horses had been killed during the fighting. Horses gave the Spaniards a great advantage in battle. Their loss could not be replaced.

As the explorers surveyed the devastated village, Indian captives told Juan Ortiz that Spanish ships had been seen in a harbor just 80 miles away. Were these the brigantines commanded by Francisco Maldonado, bringing supplies to de Soto? But the adelantado ordered Ortiz not to tell anyone. He was afraid that if the soldiers learned the ships were nearby, they would want to return to Cuba. De Soto knew that if he and his troops returned now–hungry, wounded, and empty-handed–he would never be able to mount another expedition to Florida.

De Soto left his ships to fend for themselves and ordered his party–now fewer than 600 men–to march north, away from the coast. They would have to find a winter camp.

During November and December, de Soto's party traveled nearly 150 miles northwest. They finally stopped in an abandoned Indian town, Alibamu, and settled in for the winter. They met with the local Chickasaw Indians. Initially, the natives were friendly, but relations soon worsened.

In March 1541, Hernando de Soto and his men prepared to set out again. He insisted on taking 200 Chickasaw as porters. Although their chief agreed, the adelantado was suspicious. He posted a guard and told his men to sleep fully armed.

His fears were well-founded. Early one morning, Chickasaw warriors silently converged on the Spanish camp. When they attacked, whooping and firing flaming arrows, the explorers were unprepared. They ran in all directions, making easy targets for the Indians. De Soto, who had slept in his armor, and a handful of other soldiers were finally able to mount a counterattack that drove the Indians back.

It was a terrible defeat for de Soto's men. Twelve Spaniards had been killed, along with about 50 horses and most of their hogs. Their winter camp had been burned to the ground by the natives' arrows. Many of their weapons had been damaged in the fire. For example, the long wooden handles of

This 16th-century drawing shows Indians attacking a village with flaming arrows. The Chickasaw attack on de Soto's camp was a disaster for the Spanish.

the deadly lances that the foot soldiers used were destroyed.

By now the exploring party was down to about 450 men. The survivors made camp nearby, where they set up a forge and went about repairing the weapons and equipment they had salvaged from the fire. The weather was cold and wet. The miserable explorers were hungry, and their clothes were badly worn. They shivered through the chilly nights. At any moment, they expected an Indian attack. Fortunately for the Spaniards, the Chickasaw waited for more than a week. When they did attempt another night raid, the Spaniards were ready. This time, they routed the Indians.

In April 1541, de Soto's army headed west. Traveling was slow because many soldiers were sick or wounded. The Indians continued to attack, killing 15 Spaniards in one battle. At this point, the expedition did not have any direction. The explorers were just wandering around the countryside.

As the Spaniards looked across the Mississippi, 200 canoes filled with warriors approached the party. The leader spoke briefly with de Soto, but the peaceful meeting ended when nervous Spanish crossbowmen fired on the canoes, killing six Indians, and the natives withdrew.

On May 9, 1541, Hernando de Soto and his men came upon the Mississippi River. The adelantado was amazed at its size. He called it the Great River.

Although there were hostile Indians living along the shores of the Mississippi, de Soto and his men decided to camp along the river. For the next month, the soldiers cut down trees. They used the lumber to build four wooden barges. On June 18, the Spaniards loaded their horses and supplies onto the barges and crossed the river.

De Soto's men spent the summer and fall wandering through the area that today is western Arkansas. As winter approached, the men moved into an Indian village. They had food and warm homes, and they built a stockade around the village to discourage attacks. However, it was a hard, cold winter. Many men died. Among them was Juan Ortiz, de Soto's interpreter.

As the spring of 1542 approached, the Spaniards were tired of exploring. More than half of de Soto's men were gone. Most had been killed by Indians or disease, but others had run away. He had started with 230 horses, but only 40 remained. De Soto decided to return to the Mississippi River when the weather improved. There, he planned to build two boats and sail down the river to Mexico with his weary soldiers. Hernando de Soto's quest for gold in Florida was a failure.

Night falls over the Mississippi. (Inset) In an eerie midnight ceremony, Hernando de Soto's dead body is lowered into the river.

Death of the Adelantado 6

*I*n March 1542, the weary Spaniards started back toward the Mississippi River. By the time they reached the banks of the mighty river two months later, de Soto was very sick. He may have been suffering from **malaria**, a deadly disease that causes chills and high fever. The adelantado knew that he would not survive the expedition. He called his officers to his bedside, thanked them for their loyalty, and appointed Luis Moscoso as his successor. On May 21, 1542, Hernando de Soto died.

If the natives knew the feared Spanish leader was dead, they might attack. So the Spaniards buried de Soto at night. Then they marched their horses over his grave to hide it from the Indians. However, Moscoso suspected that the natives knew where the feared adelantado was buried. In the middle of the next night, the Spaniards dug up de Soto's corpse, wrapped it in a weighted cloth, and sank it in the middle of the Mississippi River.

With de Soto's death, the Spaniards abandoned the plan to float down the Mississippi. Instead, they would try to walk to Mexico. With luck, Moscoso reasoned, they might still find riches. From June until October, the army wandered west. They lived off the land and fought the Indians as they traveled.

Finally, Moscoso halted the march. He decided to march back to the Mississippi, make boats, and float to Mexico–de Soto's original plan. For the next two months, the starving army retraced its steps. By the time the soldiers reached the river in December, they had traveled nearly 800 miles.

During the winter, spring, and early summer of 1543, the men built seven crude brigantines. Early in July, the surviving members of de Soto's expedition–fewer than 350 men–boarded the boats.

As they sailed down the river, the Spaniards often stopped at Indian towns and took whatever food they needed. As a result, they were under constant attack. The Indians kept up the fighting until the boats were nearly at the Gulf of Mexico.

Once out of the river, the soldiers sailed for about a month before reaching Pánuco, a Spanish settlement in Mexico. "Many, leaping on shore, kissed the ground; and all, on bended knees, with hands raised above them, and their eyes to heaven, remained untiring in giving thanks to God," wrote one survivor. The 311 half-starved, haggard survivors had traveled approximately 3,000 miles on land and another 1,100 miles over water.

Eventually, many returned to Spain. About half decided to stay in the New World, either in Peru or in Mexico.

And so, the expedition of Hernando de Soto ended in failure. Or so it seemed to the king of Spain and to others. After all, de Soto did not find gold. He did not establish a settlement in Florida. His men had not converted the Indians to Christianity. In fact, his hostile relations with the Native Americans would make life more difficult for future Spanish explorers and Christian missionaries in the New World. And the lengthy and disappointing journey certainly did not bring him personal glory.

But de Soto's expedition did have a positive impact on Spain. At the same time that de Soto's men were marching through the South, another Spanish conquistador was seeking the Seven Cities of Gold in the West. When Francisco Coronado returned without finding gold or silver either, Spanish hopes of untold riches in the New World were shattered. From this point forward, the Spanish began developing the resources at hand in Mexico—mines, sugar and cotton plantations, and ranches. This would bring wealth to Spain in the short term and forever change the region and its people.

Survivors of de Soto's expedition wrote about La Florida. Their rich accounts led others to want to settle there. Twenty-three years after the adelantado's body slipped beneath the waves of the Mississippi River, Pedro Menéndez de Avilés founded a Spanish settlement at St. Augustine. Today, it is the oldest continuously occupied city in North America.

And although Hernando de Soto did not gain riches for his exploration of Florida, he did earn the glory he sought. Today, he is remembered as the first European to see the Mississippi River and to explore the vast and varied lands that make up the southern United States.

1500 Hernando de Soto born in Jerez de los Caballeros, Spain.

1513 Juan Ponce de León lands on the east coast of Florida; Vasco Núñez de Balboa discovers the Pacific Ocean.

1514 De Soto enters service of Pedro Arias Dávila; travels to the Darién colony (Panama) in the New World.

1523 Opposes Francisco Fernández de Córdoba's attempt to take over a Central American province and is imprisoned; escapes, then helps Pedro Arias Dávila capture Córdoba.

1530 Joins Francisco Pizarro's expedition to conquer the Inca Empire in Peru, South America.

1532 Helps Pizarro capture the Inca ruler Atahualpa and conquer the capital city, Cajamarca.

1537 Receives permission from King Charles to explore and colonize Florida.

1539 Lands on the western coast of Florida and claims it for Spain; establishes settlement at Ucita and begins search for gold; abandons Ucita for winter encampment at Anhaica.

1540 Meets La Señora de Cofitachequi, a cacique who gives him pearls; crosses the Appalachian Mountains; passes through territories of the Chocktaw and Chickasaw tribes.

1541 Reaches the banks of the Mississippi River in May; crosses the river the next month and explores Arkansas; makes winter camp and decides to end expedition in the spring.

1542 Dies on May 21 of fever; buried in the Mississippi.

1543 The 311 survivors of de Soto's expedition reach Pánuco, a Spanish settlement in Mexico.

Glossary

adelantado–the title of a Spanish governor in the New World.

arquebus–a portable matchlock gun, developed in Europe during the 15th century. The arquebus was very heavy and usually was supported with a wooden staff when it was fired.

brigantine–a large sailing ship with two masts. Brigantines usually were rigged with square sails, except for a fore-and-aft mainsail.

cacique–the chief of a Native American tribe.

caravel–a sturdy sailing ship developed by the Portuguese in the 15th century. Caravels had broad hulls, a high and narrow deck at the stern (called a "poop deck"), and three masts. They usually carried both square and triangular (lateen) sails.

civil war–a war between two groups of citizens that live in the same country.

conquistador–a spanish soldier who led the conquests of Mexico, Peru, and America in the 16th century.

farrier–a person who makes shoes for horses (usually a blacksmith).

guerrilla–describes a method of warfare in which the enemy is harassed and annoyed by constant surprise attacks, rather than faced in open combat.

heathen–an uncivilized person, or, to the Spanish of de Soto's time, any person who was not Christian.

interpreter—a person who helps two people who speak different languages to communicate by translating what they are saying.

isthmus—a narrow strip of land connecting two large land areas.

litter—a platform used to carry a single person.

maize—Indian corn.

malaria—a blood disease that is carried by mosquitoes and causes severe chills and fever. Until the late 19th century, malaria was often fatal.

Moors—Arabs from North Africa who invaded Spain in the eighth century. Because the Moors followed Islam, they were involved in a series of bloody wars with the Christian people of Spain and the rest of Europe. The Moors were forced out of Spain in 1492.

mutilation—the act of cutting off or destroying a limb or essential body part.

palisade—a fence of wooden stakes around a town to defend against attackers.

patron—a person who uses his or her wealth or power to help someone else.

province—a region of a country, usually separated from other provinces for geographical or political reasons.

treason—the crime of attempting to overthrow the government or ruler to whom a person owes allegiance.

Further Reading

Cabeza de Vaca, Alvar Núñez. *The Account: Alvar Núñez Cabeza de Vaca's Relación.* Houston: Arte Publico, 1993.

Duncan, David Ewing. *Hernando de Soto: A Savage Quest in the Americas.* Norman: University of Oklahoma Press, 1997.

Ewen, Charles R., and John H. Hann. *Hernando De Soto Among the Apalachee: The Archaeology of the First Winter Encampment.* Gainesville: University Press of Florida, 1998.

Galloway, Patricia, ed. *The Hernando De Soto Expedition: History, Historiography, and "Discovery" in the Southeast.* Lincoln: University of Nebraska Press, 1997.

Hudson, Charles. *Knights of Spain, Warriors of the Sun; Hernando de Soto and the South's Ancient Chiefdoms.* Athens: University of Georgia Press, 1997.

Hudson, Joyce Rockwood. *Looking for De Soto: A Search Through the South for the Spaniard's Trail.* Athens: University of Georgia Press, 1993.

Lavender, David S. *De Soto, Coronado, Cabrillo: Explorers of the Northern Mystery.* Washington, D.C.: National Park Service Division of Publications, 1992.

Schell, Rolfe F. *De Soto Didn't Land at Tampa.* Fort Myers Beach, Fla.: Island Press, 1966.

Swanton, John. *Final Report of the United States: De Soto Expedition Commission* (reprint edition). Washington, D.C.: Smithsonian Institution Press, 1985.

Picture Credits

JIM GALLAGHER is the author of more than 10 books for young adults, including biographies of Vasco da Gama and Ferdinand Magellan in the Chelsea House series EXPLORERS OF NEW WORLDS. A former newspaper editor and publisher, he lives near Philadelphia.